you are perfect

JUST THE WAY YOU ARE.

Everyone is different in their own special way,

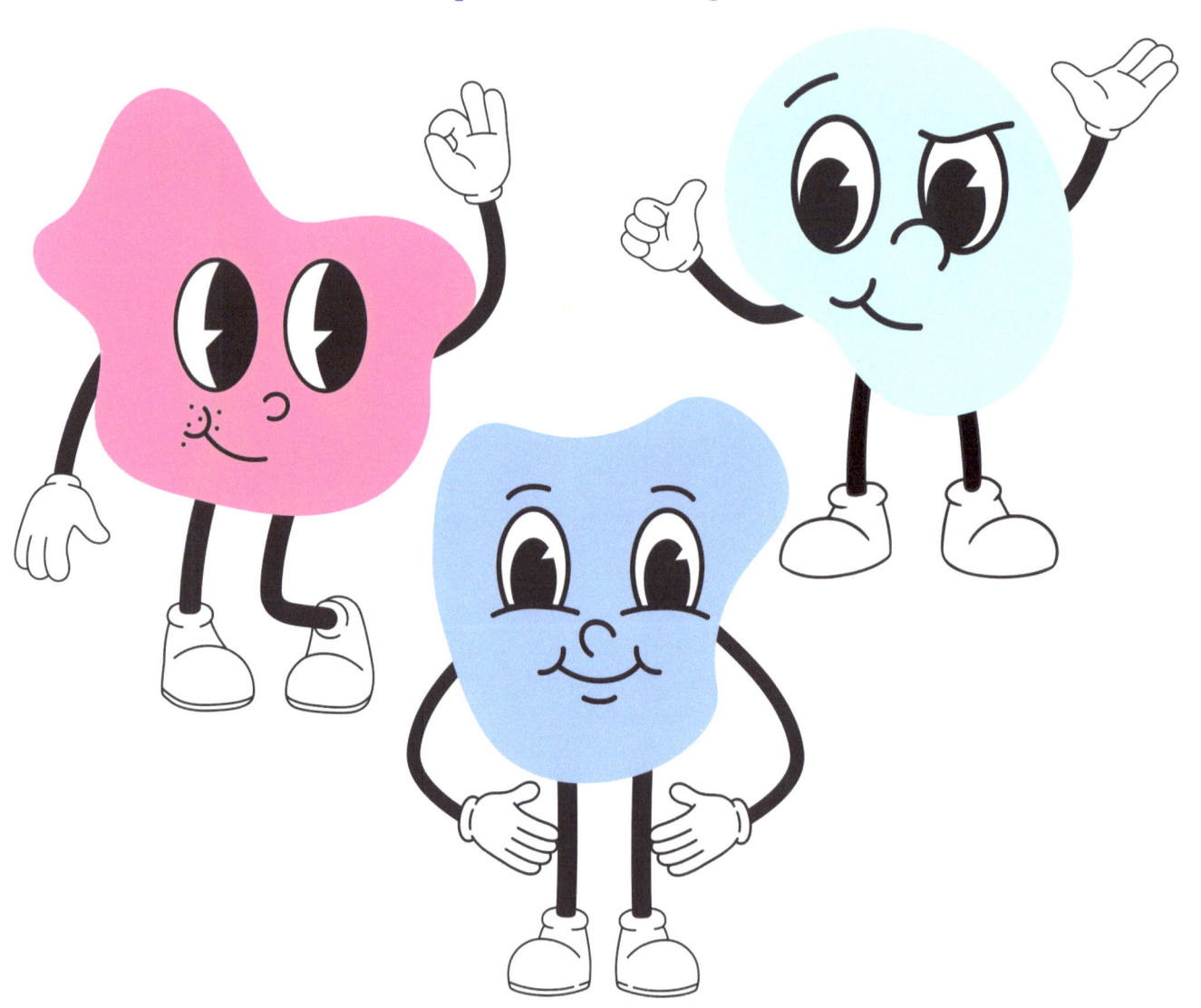

and ADHD is just one of the many beautiful ways that our brains can be different.

Meet Casey.

Casey's brain works a bit differently than their friends, and some days, that can be hard.

Casey's brain makes it a bit harder to sit still or pay attention for a long time.

It's kind of like having a super energetic and curious brain!

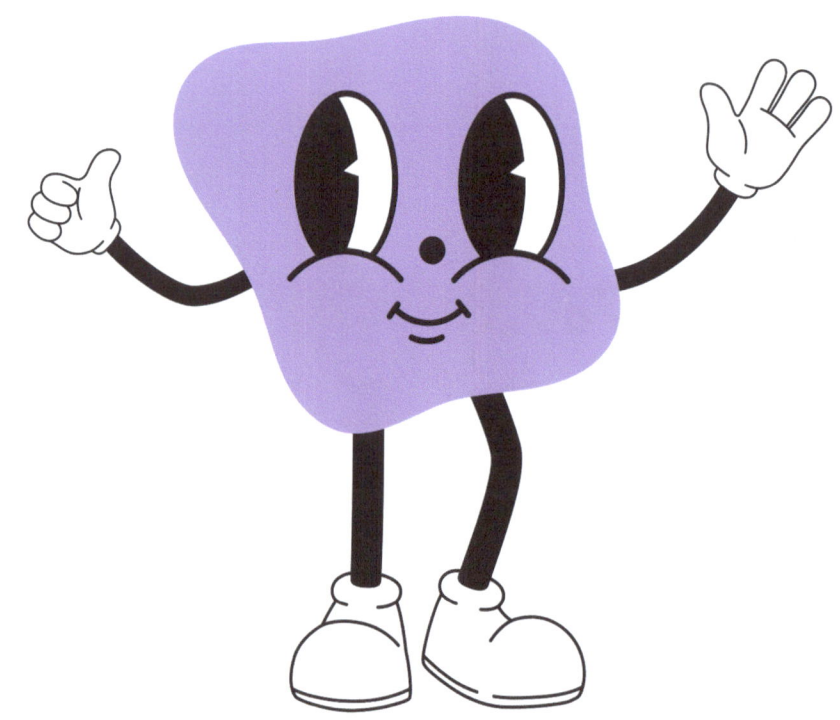

You see, Casey has ADHD
Attention Deficit Hyperactivity Disorder.

Which means their brain doesn't process information in the same way as others.

Sometimes, Casey finds it difficult to focus and keep their brain on the task at hand no matter how hard they try.

Other times, Casey's brain is so focused on one thing that it's hard to think of anything else.

Sometimes, Casey needs complete silence and zero distractions in order to focus.

Other times, Casey can't focus without lots of background noise and distractions.

Sometimes, Casey gets really frustrated with things because their brain has a hard time processing the information.

Other times, Casey gets so bored by what is going on around them that their brain wanders off into their imagination.

Some things can be hard for Casey.

**Which is why they work hard
to find tools or strategies that can help.**

When Casey finds it hard to sit still,...

they might use a band on their chair so they can move their feet while working.

When Casey finds it hard to focus because they can hear every little sound around them,

they might put on their favourite music
to help drown it out.

When Casey gets overwhelmed by all of the things they have to do,

they might use an organizer or create a list to break down all of the big tasks into little tasks, which helps them get things done.

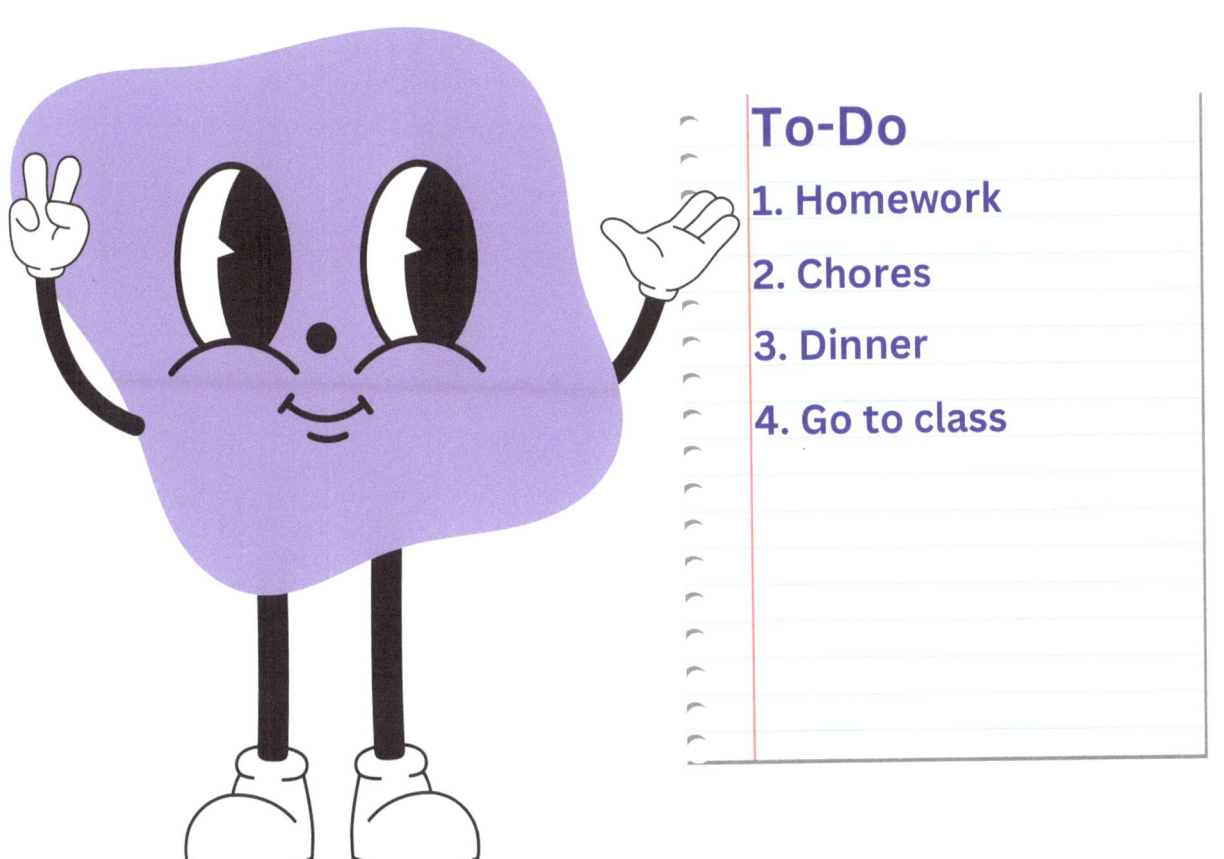

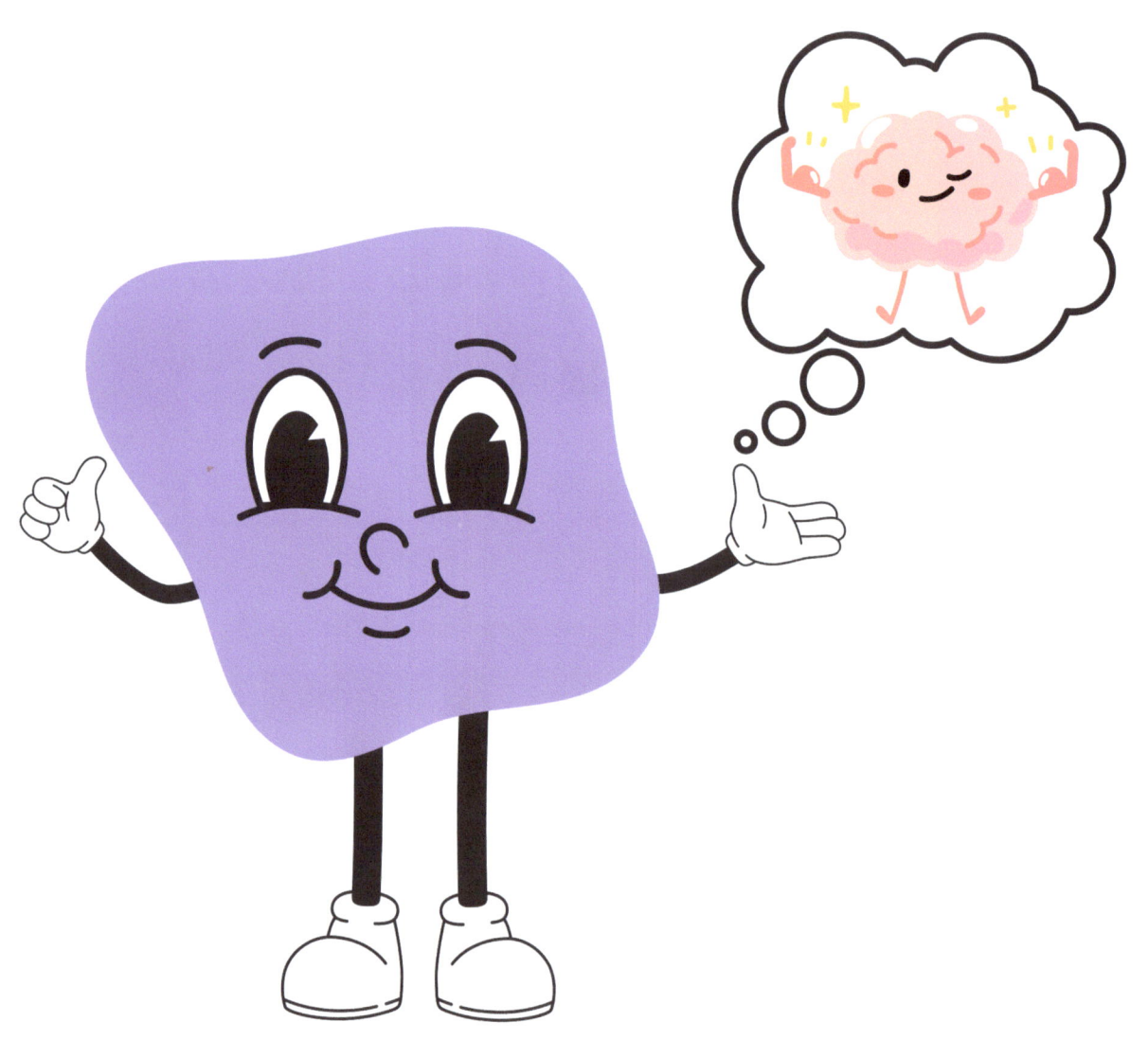

Casey knows their brain is different,
and that's ok.

Remember, having ADHD doesn't mean your brain isn't awesome.

It just means you have a super unique and fantastic brain that might need some extra understanding and support.

Just like Casey.

The End!

Visit sarafurlongauthor.com for more children's book titles.

www.ingramcontent.com/pod-product-compliance
Lightning Source LLC
Chambersburg PA
CBHW041447120626

46547CB00002B/374